A SPECIAL THANK YOU TO OUR VERY GENEROUS SUPPORTERS

Unky Mokey
Lainey Rhodes
Peggy Rhodes
Margaret Rhodes
Jay Rhodes
Lloyd Rhodes

Printed in PRC
Inkworms.com

For my children, Kiera and Ian.

Don’t just see things for what they are,
but also for what they could be.

This Book is too SMALL!

by Jason Rhodes

To
Amelia
Teddy
and Charlotte

Jason Rhodes

Inkworms

Welcome to the big, big book
of big, big animals. Let's take a look...

DANGER
Big animals ahead

On the first page we have
a big brown grizzly
whose thick fur coat
is wild and frizzly.

But wait...what’s this?
He can’t move an inch
and his little friend bunny
is in quite a pinch.

Even bigger than the grizzly
is this big wobbly moose,
whose name, I believe,
is Bumbly Bruce.

It appears that he's had
a bit of bad luck,
because on this page
his moose horns are stuck!

What now? Oh no!
This won't do at all!
This big, big book
is much too small!

The giraffe has no room
to stretch his neck out
and the ground at the bottom
is squashing his snout.

Up next is a rhino
with a bird on his back
eating gross crawly bugs
for an afternoon snack.

But the rhino's so large,
with a giant nose horn,
that the frame of his page
is split, worn and torn.

And now here's a walrus
in a bit of a pickle.
He's squashed up against
a quite sharp icicle.

This is not very good.
This won't do at all.
This big, big book
is much too small!

The biggest creature, so far,
has a trunk for a nose
which can be used to shoot water
like a big fire hose.

But now it's all kinked up
and it's just underfoot
and the elephant's honker
is completely kaput.

Helga the hippo
is all glippy and gloppy,
wading in mud
getting all kinds of sloppy.

This just won't do.
This is no good at all!
This big, big book
is much too small!

In a big, big book,
there should be room for a whale,
but this one's squished in his box,
from his head to his tail.

He has no place to go
and nothing to do,
but stay squished on this page
just being blue.

No! No! No!
This won’t do at all!
This big big book
is much too small!!!

They've all gone on strike.
They've had quite enough.
All the animals have left,
stomping off in a huff.

ON
STRIKE

But wait. What's this?
Maybe things aren't done.
With the big creatures gone,
the small ones have fun.

With the whale on the way out,
things have gotten much better
for the slippery small fish
who are happier wetter.

And Helga the Hippo
is no longer hogging
the muddy mud pit
in which she was slogging.

Now the frogs can relax
in a pool of mud bubbles
and try to forget
their froggy, frog troubles.

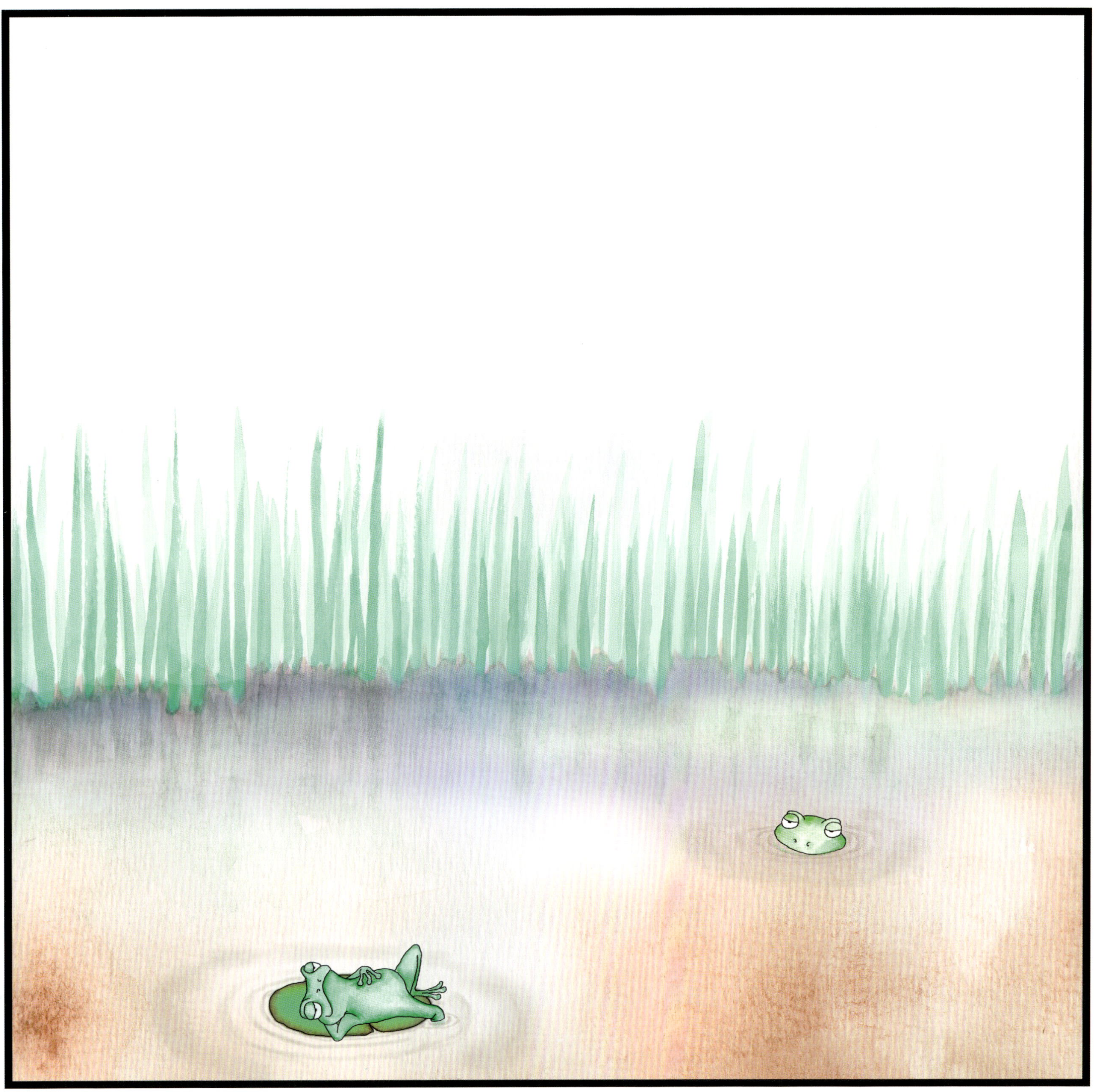

Well I guess I was wrong.
This book isn't too small.
It is big, big enough
if you're three inches tall.

With the elephant gone,
the mouse is now free
to serve his friends crumpets
and a thimble of tea.

And back in the ice cave,
the penguin has room
to skate all about,
zoom-zoomity zoom!

The penguin misses his friend.
The walrus was nice,
but now he is happy
to skate on the ice.

The rhino is gone,
way, way out of sight,
and the bird now has room,
for her flippity flight.

She can fly to and fro
and collect twigs and strings
to build a wee nest
for resting her wings.

Continuing on,
the giraffe is now gone.
His knotted up neck,
no longer blocking the lawn.

It's too bad he's left,
but on this beautiful day,
there's now plenty of room
for the meerkats to play.

Bumbly Bruce has moved on.
His horns are unstuck.
So now he can go
to his Sunday potluck.

The ducks are ecstatic.
They have invited a goose,
because in such a small space,
you can't play duck, duck moose.

And now we have reached
the end of this book.
We are back to the bunny,
curled up in a nook.

I'm happy to say,
that after it all,
this big, big book
is perfectly small.

THE END

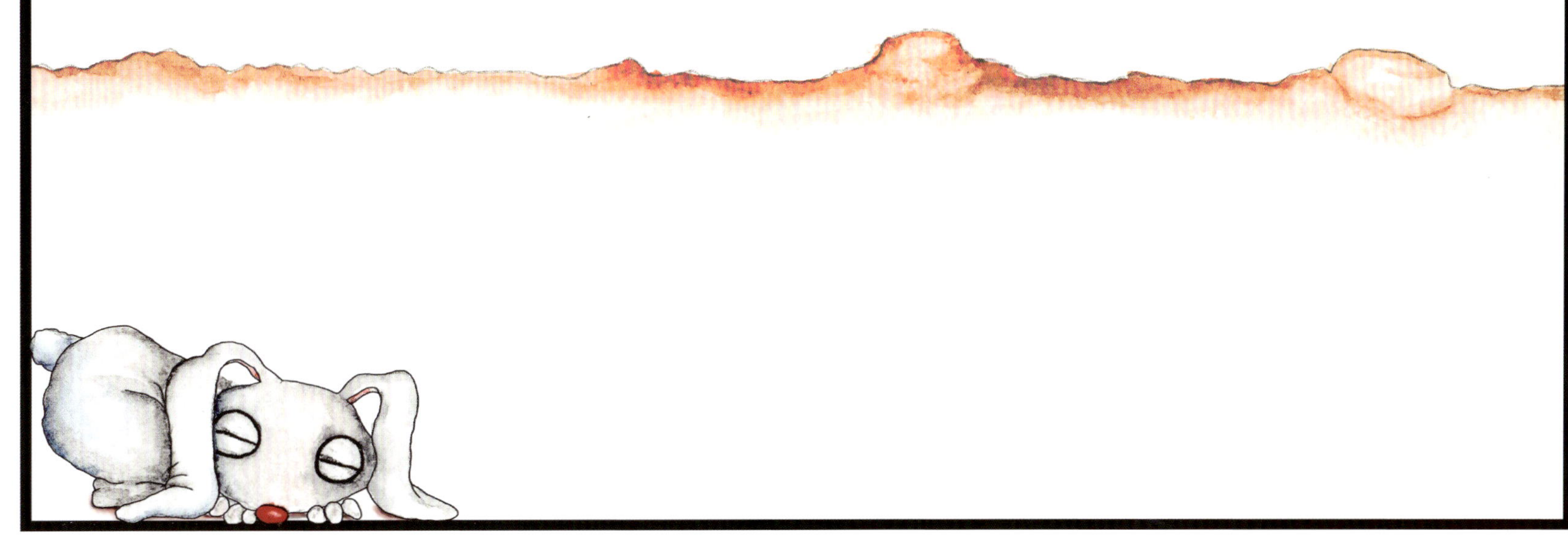